It All Depends
On Your Perceptions

There's a lot you can learn about life—just by paying attention to little things, and by noticing people others overlook. Frogs become princes. Victories emerge out of disasters.

In his whimsical style Maxie Dunnam offers lessons he has gleaned from the lives of famous people, everyday people and the world around him:

+ Everybody is somebody.
+ You should go home again.
+ Cry if you must, but laughter is better.
+ Thanks is a good word; forgiveness isn't bad either.
+ 'Silence is golden' is a tarnished expression.
+ Live until they bury you.
+ Before you search for something you desperately want, make sure you don't already have it.
+ We all need to be connected to somebody.
+ You can believe the truth about yourself, no matter how beautiful.
+ Sometimes you have to stop.

Beautifully designed, *Perceptions* is as much a pleasure to display as it is to read.

Maxie Dunnam is pastor of Christ Church (United Methodist) in Memphis, Tennessee. For many years he was World Editor of *The Upper Room* devotional guide.

D0905944

This special edition of *PERCEPTIONS* is published in memory of Richard Love Fisher, Jr., infant son of Dot and Dick Fisher, to whose friends and family the *PERCEPTIONS* ministry has meant so much.

PERCEPTIONS

OBSERVATIONS ON EVERYDAY LIFE

MAXIE DUNNAM

AUTHOR'S NOTE:
These anecdotes and thoughts come from everywhere. There is no way for me to credit all who have inspired me, or whose material I may have used without acknowledgment. Little that we say and think is original. So my thanks to those who provided a "germ" story or thought.
M.D.D.

Library of Congress Card Number: 89-81759
ISBN: 0-917851-59-5

BRISTOL BOOKS
An imprint of Bristol House, Ltd.
2201 Regency Road, Suite 301 • Lexington, KY 40503
Phone: 606/276-4583   Fax: 606/276-5365

Introduction

"This past January, after two months of severe depression, I planned to take my own life. The date was January 26, and I was on my way home from work. After a struggle all day, I decided to end it all when I got home. I was so depressed I felt I would never live the life I wanted to live. On the way home your radio program ["Perceptions"] came on. That short one-minute message changed my life forever."

The young man who wrote the letter went on to thank me profusely for "saving his life."

Every week they come—not that dramatic—but words of appreciation for "Perceptions," which is aired Monday through Friday on four radio and two television stations.

The original idea came from Durelle Durham, a layman in our congregation.

We were looking for a way to use radio in communicating our concern for people and something of the spirit of our church. We were not interested in hard-sell gospel. We wanted to reach the secular audience—those who are not in church on Sunday, who do not know religious language, who may be turned off by the "preaching they grew up on" or who never heard. We went to radio first because it was less expensive. We ran the 60-second message on one of the most popular radio stations at prime driving time, 5 p.m. weekdays.

"Perceptions" was an immediate success. We received calls, words of appreciation, requests for scripts, questions about our church and faith. Letters from Christians of all denominations, from non-Christians, from Jewish folks and from at least one person who identified himself as a Hindu. Countless calls came from people needing help and further words of hope.

The impact has grown. In late 1987 Mr. and Mrs. James Seabrook gave our church a significant amount of money, requesting we put our Sunday morning worship service on television. "Perceptions" had been such a success on the radio stations that we talked with the Seabrooks and asked them to allow us to use the money to run "Perceptions" on other radio stations as well as two television stations. They were very gracious, seeing the value of the idea. Again we were committed to reach people everyday, where they lived and worked, not the already-Christian who would listen to a television broadcast on Sunday morning. So "Perceptions" is now aired on four radio stations at different times during the day and on two television stations at the beginning of the day.

I could share story after story—heartwarming

ones, humbling ones such as the letter I quoted, funny ones such as the man who named his cat "Perception" and the fellow who named his dog Maxie—and the group of medical doctors consulting over a patient, with one concluding, "We could ask Dr. Dunnam his perception."

Not long ago another minister of our church and I were checking our bags at the airport. The woman at the counter recognized both my name and my voice and thanked me profusely for these radio messages. When we were getting on the plane, the man who took my ticket asked, "You're Maxie Dunnam, aren't you?" (Most ticket-takers are only interested in seeing that you are boarding the right flight.)

"You led my neighbor to the Lord," he continued, "through your radio program."

Then he told us how his neighbor had run over to his house one afternoon after listening to "Perceptions" and with great excitement had told him he had accepted Christ. The neighbor had been listening to "Perceptions" regularly and had come to that life-changing point of making the crucial decision to accept and follow Christ.

A less believing soul than my minister-colleague may have thought those two persons were planted. It was almost unbelievable to me, but I thanked God for the imagination of persons such as Durelle Durham and the Seabrooks; for a church that is bold in seeking new ways of communicating the gospel; for resources of modern technology; and for the confirmation of the Spirit that when we sow the word, God will bring harvest.

Almost from the beginning people have wanted a collection of "Perceptions" in book form. So here it is. My prayer is that you will find hope, meaning, joy, direction, encouragement, strength and all the other gifts God has for persons who will receive God's love.

My perception is that God is ready and willing to do for us far more than we can ask or even think. And none of us need stay where we are and the way we are if where we are and the way we are is keeping us away from God's grace.

Maxie D. Dunnam

Pete Rose, a Crummy Father?

Pete Rose's daughter got caught up in the fracas surrounding his being accused of illegal gambling. She had not lived with Pete since he and her mother divorced some years ago. One of the reasons she gave for not living with him was that he was a crummy father.

"What's she mean 'a crummy father'?" Pete responded. "I'm a great father. Why, just last week I bought her a brand new Mercedes."

Unfortunately Pete Rose is not alone in thinking that's what it means to be a good parent. To substitute things for our presence is never adequate. How many troubled young people have said to me, "My mom was not there when I needed her. My dad was always too busy—we never talked"?

But this is not just true of parent-child relationships. Relationships survive and grow as we give to each other what we all need for personal wholeness—time, attention, interest—in short, the human touch of love.

Love Is Something You Do

Some high school sophomores offered definitions of love. "Life is one thing after another! Love is two things after each other," said one. Another student wrote, "Love is the feeling in your stomach of butterflies wearing roller skates." According to Rev. Donald Shelby, the one that took the prize was this: "Love is that feeling you feel when you feel you are going to have a feeling you have never felt before."

We chuckle at that—so adolescent! But most of the people I know who are having trouble in their marriages have working definitions of love not far from these. To them, love is made up of those feelings and emotions generated by physical attractions and a desire to satisfy sexual, emotional and security needs.

But love is far more. It is decision. It is something you do—an act of will that gives itself unselfishly for the good and enrichment of another.

How are you doing in your love life?

Let the Mice Teach Us a Lesson

A few years ago Johns Hopkins University did an experiment with mice. The first group of mice was held tightly in the experimenters' hands so that they could not move at all. The mice struggled but were immobilized without being injured. Then after a set period of time, they were placed in a tub of water. They immediately sank, having learned that fighting was hopeless.

A second group of mice was held in the lab technicians' hands less tightly. The creatures were given some hope of escaping the grip of the lab technician but without being actually free. After the same length of time, they were also dropped into a tub of water. These mice immediately swam to safety.

It's a parable for us humans. If we come to believe that life's struggles and fights are useless and hopeless—we will sink. Life will beat us. As long as we remain strong in will and hope by continuing the struggle, we will never be defeated.

'He Already Owned the Painting'

William Randolph Hearst, the famous newspaper owner and multimillionaire, once saw the print of a famous painting. He decided he wanted that painting, so he hired a detective to find the original.

Several months and several thousand dollars later, the detective returned with some good news and some bad news. The good news was that he had found the painting. The bad news was that he had found it in one of Mr. Hearst's own warehouses. Hearst already owned it!

Most of us are somewhat dull, even blind, to what is already ours: love, friendship, food, health, a free land in which to live. A word of caution is in order. Don't go looking around for something you think will make you happy before you pay attention to what you already have.

The Sorrow Tree

One of our favorite pastimes is to spend time thinking about how well off other people are and how bad off we are. We have so many sorrows. We think so many bad things have happened to us. Why is it that we suffer? When John and Jane go untouched, why do we deserve to be punished in this fashion?

The Hasidic Jews have a story about the sorrow tree. According to them, on Judgment Day we will be invited to hang all of our own miseries from the tree of sorrows. When we have done that we will be given permission to walk around the tree and survey everyone else's miseries in order to select a set we like better. According to Hasidic legend, in the end we freely choose our own personal set of sorrows once more. That's a charming way of saying that when we see the suffering and sorrow of others, more often than not, we are quite happy to keep our own.

Kiss an Artist Today

A bumper sticker got my attention. "Kiss an artist today." That's easy for me—my wife and daughter are artists.

But the thought is expansive and the need universal. John Powell tells about two priests who experienced a rich and rewarding friendship. They struggled together through the wilderness of long seminary training and worked together in a community ministry.

Then one of the two friends was hit by a car and killed in front of their residence. The other knelt at the side of his old friend, gently cradled the brother's head on his arm, and before all the people who had gathered blurted out, "Don't die! You can't die! I never told you that I loved you."

It can happen to any one of us; but it need not. Before this day ends, do two things. One, tell a person you have not told recently that you love them. Two, for a person you are always telling you love, do something that will validate your words.

Faith in Death

Not long ago I visited a woman who fought a raging battle with cancer. I'd seen her gritted-teeth stubbornness, had watched her refuse to be emotionally beaten down by this energy-sucking attack on her body, had witnessed a beautiful woman refusing to be humiliated by this force that ravaged her physical appearance. Today there was something different about her. Subtle, but distinctly different.

"How are you?" I asked.

Immediately she responded, "I'm praying, and I want you to pray that Jesus will come soon and deliver me." We did that together.

It wasn't a surrender to despair; it was a yielding to certain hope. It was her ultimate commitment. For more than a year she had fought a courageous battle and lived in the strength of her faith. Now she had moved to another level of commitment. She prayed confidently and in hope.

I think often of Libby and ponder how I would face my own death. I'm cultivating the kind of faith she witnessed to, believing it will give me the same courage and triumphant hope. I invite you to do the same.

Say Yes by Saying No

Have you ever realized that the best way to say *yes* to something is to say *no* to its counterpart?

There is an interesting expression of it in the New Testament. The apostle Paul said, "Do not get drunk with wine, which will only ruin you; instead, be filled with the Spirit." (Ephesians 5:18 TEV)

It works! You can eliminate the *negative* by *accentuating* the positive. The best way to get rid of a *bad* habit is to replace it with a *good* one.

William Glasser has written a book on this dynamic which he calls "positive addiction."

What are some things to which you might become positively addicted:

    physical exercise
    good eating habits
    deliberate unselfishness
    refusing to repay evil with evil
    holding back rather than jumping to conclusions
    refusing to believe the worst by holding to the best
    It's a good discipline . . . learning to say *yes* by saying *no*.

The Beautiful Truth About Me

A while ago my wife, Jerry, attended a women's retreat led by Sister Susan. A few days after returning from the retreat, Jerry received a letter from Sister Susan which was concluded with this prayer: "Oh God, help me to believe the truth about myself no matter how beautiful it is."

What a prayer! Does it shock you?

"O God, help me believe the truth about myself no matter how beautiful it is."

Hard to pray, isn't it? Hard because unfortunately even the message of Christianity, the most affirming of all religions, has come through as *self-denial*. To be sure, there is a place for *self-denial*, but that must *not* be seen as *self-depreciation* or any form of *devaluating self*.

Write the prayer down—memorize it. Pray it daily—it will change your life. "O God, help me believe the truth about myself no matter how beautiful it is."

Two Hundred Lifeguards

Can you imagine a person drowning in the presence of 200 lifeguards? Well it happened. In August 1985, 200 lifeguards with the New Orleans Recreation Department gathered at a city pool to celebrate. It was the first summer in memory that there had not been a drowning at one of the New Orleans city pools.

While they were celebrating, a 31-year-old man, Jerome Moody, drowned in that very pool.

Isn't it ironic that the 200 experienced lifeguards celebrating the fact that they had had a trouble-free season, would have a man drown in their presence?

Is there a lesson in that for us? What about our families or our close network of friends? Do we take them for granted? Is someone we know drowning from loneliness? Is a friend's marriage breaking up, and we're not paying much attention? As parents are we too busy celebrating the good in our families that we are overlooking one member desperately needing special attention?

An Image Can Be a Terrible Thing

 Peter Ustinov is one of the great actors of our day. I don't know much about him, but I was impressed by an interview of some years ago during the filming of the movie, *Death on the Nile*. He was talking about the images actors have to live with. An image is an awful thing, he said. An actor says, "I'm going to do this or that." And someone will say, "What about your image?" Ustinov said, "I don't know what my image is. I don't want to know."

And then he continued, "It is a sad state when the man looking at you in a mirror is more important than the man looking into the mirror."

If you are overly concerned about your image—if you are preoccupied with the impression you are making on other people—the chances are that you are not certain of your identity. You don't quite know who you are—and, more seriously, you are not yet the person God created you to be.

Buttons, Buttons. How Many Buttons?

Men, if you are wearing a coat, look down at your wrist. Women, use your imagination. How many buttons are there on the sleeve?

Do you know why the buttons are there? Many years ago it was very fashionable for men to wear an additional frilly cuff, and the cuffs were attached to the coat sleeve with buttons. Somewhere along the way men gave up the idea of wearing frilly cuffs, but we still have our buttons.

Isn't that the way life is? We carry around with us things that were once important but don't matter anymore. The tragedy is that many of us order our lives, establish our values and spend our energy without really asking, "For what purpose?"

We live life by default. Think about it. Do the buttons on the sleeves of your life mean anything?

'Show Him Your Tooth, Albert'

Two small boys went into the dentist's office one day and waited for the dentist to get through with his appointment. When he came into the waiting room, the older of the two boys spoke up. "Doctor, I want a tooth taken out, and I don't want any gas, and I don't want it deadened because we're in a hurry. The doctor smiled and said, "Well, you're quite a brave young man. You want a tooth pulled, and you don't want any gas, and you don't want it deadened." And the little boy said, "That's right, 'cause we're in a hurry."

"Well, okay," said the dentist, "but tell me, which tooth is it?" And the little boy turned to his smaller friend and said, "Show him your tooth, Albert!"

The world is full of people like that, isn't it? People who want to see things happen and get things done, but who want someone else to pay the price and to suffer the consequences. That's not the way it works. We have to get into the dentist chair ourselves.

You Can't Get Any Bigger than I Can!

Sir Edmund Hilary was the first person to conquer Mt. Everest. The first time he tried, he failed. He was knighted by the Queen of England, and at that gala occasion, on the wall behind the head table, was a huge picture of Mt. Everest. The people gave him a standing ovation for even daring to attempt the climb. When they ceased applauding, Hilary turned his back to the audience, faced that picture of the awesome mountain and said, "Mt. Everest, you have defeated me once and you might defeat me again. But I'm coming back again and again, and I'm going to win because you can't get any bigger, Mt. Everest, and I can."

What an attitude! What a difference it would make if we would say when we face the mountains in our own lives, "You may defeat me once, you may defeat me twice, but you're not going to defeat me forever. I'm coming back, and I'm going to win, because you can't get any bigger, and I can!"

Does Your Dog Bite?

 A fellow went up to the desk in the hotel lobby to register. A large dog lying in front of the desk made him nervous. The desk clerk greeted him. Uneasy, the man asked, "Does your dog bite?"

The desk clerk simply said, "No." With that assurance the man decided he would pet the dog. Just as he put his hand down, the dog bit him sharply. In pain, he said, "I thought you said your dog wouldn't bite."

"I did."

"But he bit me!"

I like the desk clerk's response: "Sir, that's not my dog."

It's important to ask the right questions. The questions we ask determine the answers we get. One question we ask God is, "Why are you punishing me this way?" The truth is, God isn't punishing us. We need to ask, "What do you want to teach me in this?"

So, examine the questions you ask. Instead of why—why is this happening to me? Ask, what could I learn from this experience?

If I Had It to Do Over Again

A group of sociologists conducted a survey among a group of 50 elderly people at a retirement home. Each was asked to complete an open-ended sentence. "If I had it to do over again, I would _____ ."

Three answers emerged. One, I would reflect more. Two, I would risk more. Three, I would do more things that would live on after I am dead.

Good lessons. How reflective are you? Do you move through life at such a hectic pace that you never stop to ask what does all this mean? Is God trying to say something to me in these circumstances?

What about risk taking? Do you prefer the hell of a predictable situation rather than risk the joy of an unpredictable one? And the clincher question:

What are you doing that will be remembered after you are dead? Will the memories bring joy or sadness? Appreciation or concern? How many folks will be able to say, "I'm so glad my path crossed his"?

 ## Back to the Church for Potato Salad

Tony Campolo tells about the black Baptist church he attends in Philadelphia that celebrates student recognition day once a year. After a few students had spoken, the pastor stood and said, "Young people, you may not think you're going to die, but you are. One of these days, they'll take you to the cemetery, drop you in a hole, throw some dirt on your face and go back to the church and eat potato salad."

What a sermon opener.

But what an unforgettable underscoring of the fact of death. After I had preached at the funeral of an inspired and inspiring person, a fellow said to me, "The problem is when you have my funeral, you won't have all those wonderful things to say."

My response was, "Well, you yet have time to change that. Begin to live now in such a way that I won't be on the spot when I preach your funeral."

Something for all of us to think about.

CHRIST UNITED METHODIST CHURCH
4488 POPLAR AVENUE
MEMPHIS, TENNESSEE 38117

A Good Word: Thanks

At the peak of his career, Mark Twain earned $5 a word for the magazine articles he wrote. Some wag sent Twain a $5 bill with this note: "Dear Mr. Twain: Please send me a good word."

On a sheet of paper Twain responded with one good word: "Thanks!"

Thanks *is* a good word because being grateful keeps our perspective clear. When we say thanks we acknowledge that we can't make it on our own. We are dependent on others.

Thanks is a good word also because being grateful opens us to happiness and to God. A young woman with a crippling disease was left paralyzed and almost voiceless. An insensitive social worker asked her one day if she wouldn't just as soon be dead. The girl, with a radiant face, whispered from her wheelchair, "I would not have missed being alive for anything. I thank God for every minute—even the most impossible ones."

If you want to give someone a good word, say "Thanks."

Damaged Trees in the Human Orchard

Harry Emerson Fosdick told of a curious practice of apple growers in the state of Maine. A friend, visiting an orchard one day, saw the trees laden with apples to the point that the branches had to be propped up to keep them off the ground. When he exclaimed about it, the owner said, "Go, look at the tree's trunk near the bottom." He saw that the tree had been badly wounded with a deep gash. "That is something we have learned about apple trees," said the owner of the orchard. "When the tree tends to run to wood and leaves and not to fruit, we wound it, gash it, and almost always—no one knows why—this is the result; it turns its energies into fruit."

Close observation will show that we know many wounded trees in the human orchard of whom this is a parable—those who experience intense suffering, but in their suffering discover the great realities of life and begin to produce the fruit of the Spirit. The trouble with most of us is that "we want to get to the promised land without going through the wilderness."

27

 ## In-Between People

A young man recently said to me, "I can't talk to my parents any more. They don't listen, much less understand. What am I to do?"

A teenage girl ran away from home and wrote this letter: "Dear Mom and Dad: I hate you, but I love you. I need you and then I despise you. I wish you would die, but then I would feel guilty like I always do! Why can't I understand you like I want you to understand me?"

A woman agonized in a recent counseling session, "But I don't want a divorce—please help me!"

The need and the plea are loud and clear. Estrangement exists, not only between individuals, but the ruptures in our society are also obvious.

The Cotton Patch Version of the New Testament has this word from St. Paul: "God was in Christ putting his arms around the world and hugging it to himself." That's what persons need to do—to be in-between people—bridges of reconciliation.

Love Is Awareness

 Down in Mississippi where I grew up we had a quaint way of describing a beginning courtship. "John is paying attention to Mary."

Pretty descriptive. A friend told me that for about three years he had intentionally sought the meaning of love. He talked about it with preachers and philosophers, with the educated and uneducated.

The most helpful definition came from a workman in a furniture factory. "Love is awareness," the fellow said. That became a key for exciting living for my friend and has turned him into one of the most sensitive, alive and affirming people I know.

That's not everything love is, but love *is* that—awareness.

A recent study indicated that some of the loneliest persons are married couples. They have nice homes, good jobs, money, family—everything, but they are out of touch with each other. Love means relationship. Relationship requires awareness. So the answer to our deepest need for love begins in awareness, in paying attention.

Speak the Word of Forgiveness

The young girl is bright, talented and—until three years ago—was almost a model child. Then she began to rebel—drug involvement, skipping school, running away from home and total rejection of her parents.

You can imagine the parents' desperation and despair, the pain and powerlessness and of course, the *guilt* and feelings of failure.

In a long-distance telephone conversation, the mother was sobbing as she shared her grief and guilt. You could almost feel the pain throbbing through the telephone receiver. I knew that she was taking the burden of sin upon herself—the burden of her own real or imagined failure. Clearly and with conviction, I said, "In the name of Christ, you are forgiven."

I could feel the quiet come over her, and I could sense the relief and release that she was experiencing. The tone of her voice changed as she said, "Thank you, oh, thank you."

People around you need to hear that word—forgiveness—and you can speak it.

A Deficiency of Thought

If I had to pick a word to describe our time, high on the list—if not at the very top—would be the word *bored*. Clifton Fadiman has described our boredom as a special kind: "Not unhappiness, not fatigue . . . but that odd modern stunned look that comes from a surfeit of toys and a deficiency of thoughts."

He got us, didn't he? Think about that in light of the daily routine interests of your life.

A *surfeit of toys*: With what do you surround your life? And for what purpose?

A *deficiency of thought*: What challenging ideas have you pursued lately? What probing possibilities for growth have you been considering?

To be a whole person, and to overcome our boredom, two things are essential:

One, a faith to live by.

And two, a cause to live for.

Without these we will continue to betray our emptiness with that "odd modern stunned look that comes from a surfeit of toys and a deficiency of thought."

Sam Rayburn—Bonham, Texas

When Speaker of the House Sam Rayburn was near the end of his life and discovered just how ill he was, he surprised his colleagues in Congress by announcing that he was going home to Bonham, Texas. Why go to such a not-even-on-the-map kind of place for medical tests and treatment when the best medical facilities of the world were available to him?

Rayburn told them why. "Bonham, Texas," he said, "is a place where people know it when you are sick and care when you die."

Other persons as channels of God's love are essential for our life's journey.

When a person loves me in spite of myself; when I am loved though undeserving; when I have hurt another deeply or have been calloused to another's feelings and needs; when I have been insensitive to the pain and reaching-out of another—yet loved and accepted, I experience this as God's love for me. I hope it's the same with you.

As Far North As Possible

A university freshman was about to have her first blind date. Her roommate was making all the arrangements and asked whether she preferred Southern boys or Northern boys. A Midwesterner, she was innocently unaware of such subtle distinctions and asked what the difference was.

Her worldly-wise roommate answered, "Southern boys are more romantic. They will take you walking in the moonlight and whisper sweet nothings in your ear. Northern boys are more active. They like to go places and do exciting things."

The girl pondered the contrast and then asked wistfully, "could you please find me a Southern boy from as far North as possible?"

The story suggests our lack of decisiveness, our desire to have everything the way we want it.

It can't be. Life on earth is life in the making, involving constant choice and frequent conflict.

As we choose we need to ask two questions:

One, does my choice offer meaning beyond today—beyond momentary gratification?

Two, will what results be good for others as well as for myself?

Mom Says, 'Everything Is O.K'

I was spending the night in the hospital room with my mother. Fifteen years before, she had won a tough, ravaging battle with cancer. Now it had struck again. She had had a mastectomy that morning and had been sedated all day. In the middle of the night I was dozing, but her stirring brought me to alertness. I had the feeling that she wanted to talk, and that she wanted to talk about *real* things, not just make time-passing conversation.

How did she feel? What was she thinking? There was a lot of deep sharing. I hope I never forget that night and what she said. "When you give your life to the Lord, Son, everything has to be all right—no matter what happens." It was her way of expressing confidence that she was o.k. in God's hands. She had known God's love and care in the past, and she could trust him now.

Mom taught me that trust is a verb. We trust and rely on God to be true to his promises.

Dying of a Broken Heart

Loneliness is the number one physical killer in America today. That's what Dr. James Lynch, medical researcher at Johns Hopkins, contends in his book, *The Broken Heart.*

Using actuarial tables from 10 years research, Dr. Lynch says that those who live alone—single, widowed, divorced—have premature death rates from two to ten times higher than individuals who live with others. Living alone, he says, does not necessarily produce loneliness, but the two are often related. Among divorced people, suicide is five times higher, fatal car accidents four times higher.

People who live alone visit physicians more frequently than do married people, and they stay in hospitals twice as long for identical illnesses.

What does all this say? Dr. Lynch convincingly argues that loneliness produces physical illness and that people literally die of broken hearts.

What lonely person do you know for whom you may be the preventive medicine of hope and life?

The Only Thing that Has Roots

A 19-year-old young man hanged himself. Those who found him discovered a note tacked to the tree beside his body. It read, "This tree is the only thing I have found in life that has any roots."

Dramatic? Yes! Overly so? No!

I doubt if there is one of us who does not know someone in desperate need of security—roots—a feeling of belonging, a sense of being connected.

More and more I am convinced that the breakdown of the family is our most devastating national problem. This breakdown leaves people adrift, with no roots. That's the reason the religious community must provide fellowship and identity. That's the reason intentional friendship is essential.

Do you know someone looking for security and belonging? Don't let them think that some tree is the only thing they can find with roots.

 Loved, No
Matter What

During a terrible period of his political career, Theodore Roosevelt discovered life's pressures to be almost unbearable. He told of an evening when things were looking mighty low—until he came home, and Edith, his wife, met him at the door. In a letter to his sister, he shared his feelings:

"As I went up the stairs, I suddenly realized that after all, no matter what the outcome of the election, my happiness was assured—that even though my ambition to have the seal of approval put upon my administration might not be gratified, my happiness was assured—for my life with Edith and my children constitutes my happiness."

It is a source of great strength and support to have family and friends who stand with us no matter what. Greater yet, is the confidence that what we do is for the good of humankind and is in keeping with God's will.

Not enough of us stop to ask about the consequences of our actions, and certainly not enough of us cultivate our family and core friendships enough to give us the confidence that we are loved no matter what.

'Never Again the Same'

The philosopher Berdwaev was at a concentration camp more than 40 years ago when the Nazis were murdering Jews in the gas chambers. At one point a distraught mother refused to part with her little baby. The officer tussled with her, trying to split them apart because he needed only one more Jew to throw in the gas chamber to fulfill his quota for the day.

And then it happened. Another woman, a simple woman named Maria, realized what was happening. In a flash she pushed the mother and her baby out of the way, and she became the one thrown by the officer into the chamber!

"At that moment," said Berdwaev, "I saw the power of Christ at work in the world for the first time, and I knew that never again could I be the same person!"

That's dramatic, but it raises a question. Have we ever done anything so powerful in demonstration of love and courage that it made a difference in someone else's life?

The Salvation Army

The Salvation Army is one of the great caring ministries in the world, and well it might be. Its founder, General William Booth, went blind in his later years. His son, Bramwell, broke the news to him. "You mean I'm blind?" The General asked.

"I fear that we must contemplate that," his son replied.

"I shall never see your face again?" asked the General.

"No, probably not in this world," the son replied.

The old man's hand moved across the counter and grasped his son's. "Bramwell," he said, "I've done what I could for God and for people with my eyes. Now I shall do what I can for God and for people without my eyes."

We will never be defeated in life if we take control of our circumstances, rather than allowing them to control us.

It's Not Over Till It's Over

Do you remember Yogi Berra, one of the greats of baseball? One of his great theological statements was "It's not over till it's over."

Yogi was right. Baseball teaches us that in all sorts of ways. In 1986, for instance, Bob Brenley, catcher for the San Francisco Giants, set a major league record *with four errors* in one game against the Atlanta Braves.

In that same game, he came up to bat in the ninth inning. The count was three balls and two strikes—the last inning. Do you know what happened? Bob Brenley, in that game in which he had set a world record for errors, hit a home run and won the game for San Francisco, seven to six.

You see, it's never over till it's over. In theological circles, we talk about grace. Grace means you always have another chance. Each one of us has the chance to live as though what happened in the past doesn't matter.

# The Support We Need

The way to get help is to ask for it. Everybody needs someone to hold them up and to encourage them when they face pain and adversity.

When Nathaniel Hawthorne came home in utter despair and failure after losing his job in the Customs House, his wife responded, "Now you can write that book you have always wanted to write." Under that kind of uplifting support, Hawthorne wrote *The Scarlet Letter*, one of the greatest pieces of literature the world has ever known. The truth is there is someone there, *for each of us*, who will perform that saving work in our life—if we will get beyond our self-sufficient pride and share with another one who is willing to listen and to care.

The way to get help is to ask for it—at least let someone know we need it. Also, each of us can be that needed source of encouragement for another.

Sometimes You Have to Stop

Displayed in the British Museum in London is the final draft of Thomas Gray's masterpiece poem, "Elegy Written in a Country Churchyard." Lovers of English literature marvel at how every word seems to be carefully chosen.

The amazing thing is that Thomas Gray never considered that poem complete. In the display you can see his process, each successive draft carefully penned by hand. Seventy-five of them! And the author was still unsatisfied.

There are two lessons here. One, there's always room for improvement. If we are perfectionists, that will likely drive us almost crazy. If we are not perfectionists, we need to remember consistently to do our best.

The second lesson is that the time comes when we have to move on, leaving both success and failure behind us. St. Paul put it this way in the New Testament: "One thing I do, forgetting what lies behind, and straining forward to what lies ahead, I press on toward the goal."

You can relax, knowing that maybe your best is not good enough—but you'll have another chance.

Gretzky on Responsibility

 Wayne Gretzky, known to professional hockey fans as "The Great Gretzky" was being interviewed a few years ago. The interviewer pointed out that at age 23 Gretzky was already a multimillionaire, had already broken most of the sport's records and would go down in history as one of the greatest players of all time.

Then the questioner asked, "Well, Wayne, what can you possibly have to look forward to?" After a brief pause Gretzky answered, "Tonight's game."

Despite his accomplishments, he was ready to move on and do what was needed for that moment.

That's the secret of living life to its hilt—to be able to concentrate on the task at hand, the immediate responsibility to which you are called. Keep your attention on the present, and the past won't haunt you nor will the future burden you with fear.

A Chameleon and a Plaid Coat

The other day I saw a chameleon—the first I'd seen in a long time. He was as green as the leaf on which he rested. I watched him closely or I would have lost him when he moved from the leaf onto a brown limb and changed his color.

Watching that amazing creature of nature, I remembered Carl Sandburg's story about the chameleon who did well changing its colors to match his environment until one day he accidentally crawled onto a scotch plaid sport coat. He had a nervous breakdown heroically trying to relate to everything at once.

I know some folks who are stressed out, tension-ridden, depleted of self-identity, bereft of self-confidence because they are trying to be all things to all persons.

People were never meant to be chameleons. Why don't you quit trying?

'If I Were Your Wife I'd Poison You'

One day Lady Astor said to Winston Churchill, "Mr. Churchill, if I were your wife I'd poison your tea." He replied, "Madam, if I were your husband, I should drink it."

Then there was the time when George Bernard Shaw sent two tickets for his new play to Churchill with this note: "These are two tickets for the opening night of my new play, one for you and one for a friend . . . if you have one." Churchill, not to be outdone, sent the tickets back with this note: "I cannot attend the opening night. Send two tickets for the next night, if there is one."

I often think that what the world needs is not all of Churchill's other marks of greatness, but his capacity for humor. We laugh *at* people but not *with* them. Or we give people the occasion to laugh *at* us rather than *with* us.

Another problem is that we are unable to laugh at ourselves. Most of us take ourselves too seriously and think we are more important than we are.

Laughter is healing. Humor takes our minds off ourselves and relieves stress. Consider this rule for life: Cry if you must—but laugh if you can!

Lord, Make My Words Sweet

I came across a prayer recently which I've been trying to pray daily. Listen to it. "Lord, make my words sweet and tender today for I may have to eat them tomorrow."

Have you ever
had to eat your words?
verbalized suspicions that were unfounded.
shared rumors that were untrue.

accused someone hastily because you misjudged his motives.

misunderstood what a person was saying, and you lashed back in anger.

passed on a rumor only to discover it was blatantly false.

Words can hurt, even destroy. And words can hurt us when we have to eat them. Maybe you would like to join me in praying, "Lord, make my words sweet and tender today, for I may have to eat them tomorrow."

Life Is Too Short to Feel Guilty

I didn't hear that word on the lecture circuit of a famous psychologist—or read it in the latest best-selling self-help book. I didn't hear it in a sermon. It came from a bumper sticker.

Well I'm glad it was on that street bulletin board. It's what I preach every Sunday and what the Christian church has been proclaiming for 2,000 years. Life is too short to feel guilty.

Semi-religious and quasi-psychological groups flourish with followers and money, teaching what the church has forgotten to proclaim—or do not proclaim ardently enough. The message of Christianity is that Jesus came to forgive sinners.

So I'm happy when anybody, or any group, joins me in sharing that word because life is too short to feel guilty.

Guilt Is Good When It Motivates Change

We usually think about guilt as bad—something we ought to get rid of. And that's true—guilt devastates our lives, and so much guilt is unfounded. We are always taking responsibilities that don't belong to us—and when we fail in those responsibilities we feel guilty. Some people seem to soak in guilt—they feel guilty for everything that goes on—that's sick guilt.

But guilt can be healthy when it motivates change.

I heard recently of a person who went to a therapist to get rid of his guilt so he could get back to living life as he normally had. The therapist wisely said, "If you want to get rid of your guilt, stop doing what's causing it."

That's simple enough, isn't it? And it works. So remember, if you want to get rid of your guilt, stop doing what's causing it.

Count Your Resources

Do you remember Father Lawrence Jenco? He spent many long months as a prisoner of Lebanese terrorists a few years ago.

Jenco tells of how he was bound and trussed like a turkey and shoved into a rack beneath a flat bed truck where the spare tire is usually stored. Apparently his captors were taking him to a new place of hiding. Father Jenco felt certain that they were taking him out to kill him.

On that awful ride, he remembers saying these words to himself: "I am a human being of worth and dignity. I belong to God. I am redeemed."

He prayed words like these from the Psalms: "Yea though I walk through the valley of the shadow of death, I shall fear no evil, FOR THOU ART WITH ME." He remembers reflecting upon the words of Jesus, "Lo, I am with you always to the close of the age."

What resources do you have that would serve you in a time of despair or at the threshold of death?

It's Your Brother or Your Sister

There is an old rabbinic story in which the rabbi asks, "Children, how can we determine the moment of dawn, when the night ends and the day begins?"

One person responded, "When I see the difference between a dog and a sheep?"

"No," said the rabbi.

A second person said, "Is it when I can see the difference between a fig tree and a grape vine?"

"No."

"Please tell us the answer," said the students.

The old rabbi responded, "You know when the night ends and the day begins when you can look into the face of any human being and have enough light to recognize that person as your brother or your sister; when you can say, 'I see myself in you.' Up until that time it is night, and the darkness is still with us."

Wouldn't it be something if that kind of light dawned upon us all—that those with whom we come in contact day in and day out are our brothers and sisters?

Fred Snodgrass, 86, Dead

In 1974 poor old Fred Snodgrass died. The *New York Times* printed the news with this headline, "Fred Snodgrass, 86, Dead/Ballplayer Muffed Fly in 1912."

Some sports writer wouldn't let the world forget that Fred Snodgrass made a mistake in a ball game 62 years before. The writer spelled it out in detail. It was in the World Series. The batter hit a pop fly. Fred dropped the ball, making an error which set up the winning run. The next batter hit a single. The game was over, and the Giants lost.

Unfortunately the writer wrote as though Fred's life ended when he made that mistake. But it didn't. Mark Trotter reminds us that Fred went to California after baseball, settled down in a little city named Oxnard, became the mayor of that city, was a banker and a rancher and raised a family there. People loved and respected him.

Some people handle failure the way the sports writer did. They see it as the end. But life is made up of failures—and our bouncing back. No failure spells the end!

The Keepers of the Flame

Joe E. Trull tells of a primitive tribe located deep in the South American jungles. Anthropologists learned the most important role within the tribe was the "keeper of the flame." Since fire is so precious—and takes such effort to recreate—one member is entrusted with the responsibility of keeping the flame alive.

During the night the flame-keeper adds wood to the fire. He keeps the fire alive whenever the tribe moves to another location. His is a vital task.

I've begun to believe that role is the most important in every tribe and every culture—the keepers of

the flame of truth—basic integrity;

the flame of love—caring for another:

the flame of conviction—willing to stand for right and justice;

If the flame is not kept alive, values die or get distorted, and people suffer. Will you join me as a keeper of the flame?

The Compulsion Toward Perfection

A university psychiatrist tested the top salesmen of a major national insurance company. He found that those with perfection tendencies earned from $8,000 to $10,000 per year less than those who were not perfectionists. The study found that high performers are almost always free of the compulsion toward perfection. Rather than thinking of their mistakes as failures, the top salespersons have managed to learn from their mistakes and build on them.

It's a lesson most of us desperately need to learn. Too many of us are bound by a compulsion to perfection. The tragic thing is that we have been made to believe that our value is in what we do, not in who we are. Parents make that mistake with their children—affirming their performance not their person. So we end up believing we will not be accepted unless we are perfect. We don't believe in forgiveness. Listen: The compulsion to perfection will destroy us if we don't recognize and control it.

Nerd Day at High School

October 1, 1986, was declared "Nerd Day" at a Michigan high school. One freshman was bright but sensitive. Since entering high school, he had been harassed and teased for being a "nerd." One day, before "Nerd Day," this 14-year-old boy hanged himself in his own home. He simply couldn't stand the pressure any more.

Although the school will no longer have a "Nerd Day," it is too late for this boy. Was anyone sensitive to his pain before? Are we sensitive to the pain of those suffering around us now?

We may not have "Nerd Days," but for too many, every day is a "Put Down Day." They are put down, even by their friends. They may not be called nerds, but the signals they receive make them feel unwanted, uncared for, unloved.

I'm recruiting an army of people who will be sensitive to those who may be seen as misfits. Will you join me?

# The Next-Best Thing

The fellow was tired and weak all the time, drained of energy. Finally, he decided to visit his doctor. "Doctor," he said, "I feel drained and exhausted. I don't seem to have any energy. I have a chronic headache. I feel worn out all the time. What's the best thing I can do?"

The doctor knew something about the man's wild and fast-paced lifestyle. "What's the best thing you can do? You can go home after work, eat a nutritious meal, get a good night's rest and stop running around and carousing all night—that's the best thing you can do."

The man pondered for a moment, then asked, "What's the next-best thing I can do?"

Too often we decide for the next-best thing because we're not willing to pay the price for the very best. We're not willing to give up habits that are taking their toll on our physical health. We're not willing to give up activities and relationships that are morally questionable. We're not willing to pay the price of spiritual discipline. There's no point in seeking a meaningful life if we are willing only to do the next-best in finding it.

Borrowed Faith Has No Power

Somewhere recently I read this statement: "Most of the 500 wealthiest Americans got their money the old-fashioned way: they inherited it!" That may be the case with money, but it is not true with the most important things in life. It's not true of character. Of course we are influenced in character by our parents, but our own character is our own doing, our own choices, the way we choose to live.

We may inherit money, but we do not inherit faith. Someone put it in a catchy line: "God has no grand-children." Faith must be first-hand, personal, appropriated by each person. Too many of us are seeking to live on borrowed faith. The 500 wealthiest Americans may have gotten their wealth the old-fashioned way—by inheriting it— but we don't get character and faith that way. They're not inherited—they're personally claimed and cultivated.

56

Died at 30; Buried at 60

When the death of Calvin Coolidge was made public, someone quipped, "But how can they tell?"

George Bernard Shaw once said that the epitaph for many people should read, "Died at 30; buried at 60."

These sharp barbs suggest a question worth our pondering. How do you tell when a person is alive? If we can die at 30 and not be buried until we are 60, what are the signs of life and death?

You're dead when the suffering of another causes you no pain.

You're dead when your blood does not run hot in the face of blatant injustice.

You're dead when you evade truth that hurts and accept an easy lie.

You're dead when you are not willing to put forth the energy necessary to save a dying relationship.

You add to the list; if you can't, you may not yet be dead, but you are sick unto death, and you had better see a doctor.

One-Upmanship with God

I had read the story hundreds of times, but I had missed the impact of one line. It was the creation story in the book of Genesis and the line was this: "So God blessed the seventh day and hallowed it, because on it God rested from all his work which he had done in creation" (RSV).

That hit me.

No other day had God blessed. God didn't bless the day in which he separated the earth from the waters. God didn't bless the day he made the birds of the air and the fish of the sea. God didn't even bless the day he made male and female. Rather God blessed the day of rest.

That ought to say something to us workaholics, to persons who think they don't have time to rest, to play, to worship, to simply waste time renewing body, mind and spirit. It's a dangerous notion to think we can improve on God's way. If you say you don't have time to rest, you're playing one-upmanship with God.

Shaving Our Heads

I read an article in the newspaper about a young man in Milwaukee named Manuel Garcia. His hair fell out in patches because he was receiving chemotherapy for cancer. His head was shaved, and he worried about how he must appear to his friends.

When his brother, Julio, learned how upset he was about his appearance, Julio shaved his own head and then enlisted the support of 50 neighbors and relatives who did the same thing. Soon Manuel's hospital room looked like a convention site for bald headed men, and it greatly cheered him.

One thing suffering people need is for us to identify with them, to try to understand what they are going through. The very fact that we will try to do this, even though we fail, will mean far more than anything else we may do or say.

People Who Visit Art Galleries

Perhaps you have observed, as I have, two sorts of people who visit art galleries.

There are the mere vagrants who are always on the move, passing from picture to picture without seeing anything. And then there are the students who sit down and contemplate. They meditate and saturate themselves in the beauty and meaning of the art.

People's responses to life are the same. Our hectic lifestyle turns too many of us into vagrants, moving from one experience or encounter to another. We never stop to ask, "What does this mean?" or "What was John really saying?"

We do it in relation to God as well. We don't take time to simply be still and listen—to probe meaning and to ask what God may want to do with our lives.

Are you a vagrant, simply passing through the gallery? Or are you a serious looker?

No Struggle, No Growth

Experiments were done during space flights to test the effect of weightlessness on the aging process. Both carpenter ants and honeybees were used in the studies, and both species were found to age more rapidly and die more quickly in a weightless environment. It seems they needed the pull of gravity to make them work and maintain their physical vitality.

That's a parable for us humans. If things are too easy, we grow flabby. We need the difficulties to keep us strong. This awareness gives us a new way of seeing.

"This has been the period of my greatest growth in life," a fellow said to me recently. The significance of his statement was in the fact that he had lost his job six months earlier, and two months afterward his wife was diagnosed with cancer. So don't despair of the struggle you are in. Tragedy and struggle become our teachers, not our enemies.

That's His Job; What About You?

My friend Mark Trotter is a Methodist preacher. In a church he once served, there was a lady who questioned his ministry, his faith, his leadership. At times it appeared that she disagreed just to be disagreeable. He kept searching for a common ground. She wouldn't give an inch. Most of their encounters were unpleasant, but no matter how frustrated or angry she would get with him, she would always smile sweetly and say, "Just remember, Mark, God loves, and I love you."

Finally Mark got so exasperated that he said, "Please don't say that any more. I know that God loves me. Just once I'd like to hear you say, 'Mark, I love you!'"

That silenced her. Finally she said, "I can't say it," and turned and walked away.

A fellow said to someone all too glibly, "Remember, God loves you." The reply: "I know, that's his job—what about you?"

That's what people want to know. Do *we* love them?

# Sticks and Stones

"Sticks and stones may break my bones but words will never hurt me." William Ritter quoted that in a sermon and went on to make two big points.

One, words do hurt—they also heal.

Two, feelings need to be expressed. Love must be spoken.

A listener penned these words on an offering envelope in response to that preacher's sermon:

Sticks and stones are hard on bones
When cast with angry art;
And words can sting like anything,
But silence breaks the heart.

Well said. We need to speak our love out loud. Why do we ask little children how much they love us and revel at their outstretched arms as they exclaim, "The whole world full." It's not a game to be played. It's a practice to incorporate in our relationships—telling people that we care, that our love is real and as big as the world.

Cutting the Apron Strings

A young man went off to college. Apparently his mother had packed his suitcases. In the process of putting his clothing in drawers, he discovered two long narrow pieces of cloth among the shirts, socks and underwear. They were neatly folded and ironed. At first he didn't know what they were. But when he looked at the design of the cloth, he recognized the pattern. At last it came to him. These were the strings of his mother's apron. She had cut them off for him.

It's all right, parents, to be protective of your children. The proverbial apron strings may provide the security, guidance and support a child needs—but only for a season. The day comes when the strings must be cut. Someone has said it well: Our task as parents is not *only* to provide roots but also wings.

A Word for Cowards and Fools

"Failure is a word found only in the vocabulary of fools and cowards." That was the word of a commencement speaker, and I shuddered when I read it. I failed in teaching at least one of my children what it means to be financially responsible. I failed last week in seeking to bring reconciliation to a couple who are tearing each other apart emotionally. I admit my failure. Am I a coward or a fool?

That commencement speaker was wrong. Failure is not the word of the vocabulary of cowards and fools. It's the word of heroes and wise folks who keep dreaming dreams though some dreams are not realized; who keep waging battles against evil and injustice though some battles are lost; who keep throwing themselves in love and commitment into the causes of human freedom and fulfillment though many of these causes fail. The commencement speaker was wrong. I celebrate failure, not disparage it, because failure is the sure sign of attempts at greatness.

Failure Repeats Itself—Unless

Ours is a society so success-oriented that to fail makes you feel like a failure and to lose makes you a loser. We become masters of cover-up and experts at rationalization. When the United States pulled our troops from Lebanon a few years ago, the Defense Department said we "back-loaded our augmentation personnel." Then there was a father who said to his teenage son, "I'm concerned about your being at the bottom of your class." The son replied, "Don't worry, Dad. They teach the same thing at both ends."

We find any excuse possible to explain away our failure. It helps us to remember three truths.

One, failure repeats itself unless we admit it and learn from it.

Two, we need to realize that no failure is final, save our failure to accept God's grace and forgiveness.

And three, failure serves a positive purpose in our life if it causes us to turn to others for help and trust God for strength to begin again.

Someone Always Forgets

Halford Luccock once told about a young man who lived and worked in a pretty tough environment. He tried to hold on to his religion when people were cruel to him. He was not always appreciated for his religious views, and people made fun of him. They were always challenging him and his commitment. One day a particularly abusive person said, "You damn fool, can't you see if there is a God who cares a penny for the likes of you, God would tell someone to come along and give you what you need—decent food, a bed for yourself, at least a chance to make good."

The young man replied, "I reckon God does tell someone. But someone always forgets."

So God does tell someone—to feed the hungry, to clothe the naked, to provide shelter for the homeless, to visit widows, to pay attention to prisoners. God does tell someone. He tells you and me. But we forget, don't we?

Don't Judge Too Quickly

There is a story of two generals in the Civil War. The pressures of battle were intense. One general noticed that the other was visibly afraid. "Sir," he said, "if I were as frightened as you, I'd be ashamed to call myself a general in our nation's army."

"Sir," the other man replied, "if you were as frightened as I am, you would have fled the field of battle by now."

None of us knows the other person's struggles. I've never been a drinking man, so I can't begin to understand the struggle of an alcoholic. If you're not involved with people daily, as I am, then you can't understand my struggle with pretension or self-righteousness.

We need to be careful about judging another. We never know what may be going on inside. If we're not willing to be patient with people and stick with them until they are free to share their inner struggles with us, we can at least not add to their burden by judging them.

 **Everybody Is Somebody**

The clerk in a posh hotel greeted a small man who asked for a room. The fellow was so unimpressive that the clerk told him immediately no rooms were available. About that time the hotel manager came out of his office to the desk, recognized the man and called the clerk aside. He whispered to her that the man asking for the room was Pierre Monteaux, who for many years was the distinguished conductor of the San Francisco Symphony.

The clerk came back to the desk, apologized and said, "Why of course we can take care of you, Mr. Monteaux! Why didn't you tell me you were somebody?"

Whereupon Maestro Monteaux turned to leave, "Madam, everybody is somebody!"

Two lessons. One, everybody is somebody because everybody is a child of God.

Two, too many folks fall into the shameful pattern of ranking people and judging some as nobodies.

Listening: $5 for 30 Minutes

Some time ago, someone placed this ad in a Kansas newspaper. "I will listen to you talk for 30 minutes without comment for $5." We smile at that, maybe laugh. It sounds like a hoax. But the person was serious. Did anybody call? You bet they did! It wasn't long before this individual was receiving 10 to 20 calls a day. The pain of loneliness was so sharp that some were willing to try anything for a half-hour of companionship.

The truth is that every one of us encounters some person, probably daily, who would be willing to pay someone to listen. The tragedy is, we are not sensitive enough to identify them, or we don't care enough to respond. Will you start looking for those persons, and will you listen to them?

Kissing Their Ring

When John the 23rd had his first audience after becoming pope, among his first visitors was his own mother, a woman who had lived most of her life on the edge of poverty.

She marveled at the elaborate decor of the building outside Pope John's reception area. When her group was ushered inside, she noted how each person knelt to kiss the pope's ring. When her turn came she knelt also, acknowledging his spiritual authority in her life. Then she held out her hand and said, "Now, Son, you kiss this ring. For if it were not for this ring, you would not be wearing that ring!"

It's important that we keep perspective. What have you accomplished in life? Do you have a good job? Have you been successful in your profession? Do you have a happy family? Think for a moment. Who are the persons without whom these good things would not have come to you? Maybe you should be kissing their ring—I mean—do you have perspective on who has made your life what it is?

Choose Your Ruin

Some businessmen were talking at a prayer breakfast one morning. They were discussing putting their faith to work in their businesses and about making God their partner in their various enterprises. One man spoke up, "But what would happen to me if I should undertake to carry on my business as Christ teaches? Why it might mean financial ruin for me!"

There was a moment of silence when no one said anything, for everyone there knew what he was talking about. Then finally, one of the men spoke up in a soft voice. "And what will happen to you if you don't carry on your business as Christ teaches? What kind of ruin do you want?"

You can apply that question to the whole of life; not just to business, but to social relationships, to your home, to political life. What kind of ruin do you want?

Doing Beats Talking Every Time

Do you remember Dick Rutan and Jeana Yeager? They were the pilots who completed a globe-circling, non-stop flight without refueling. People said it couldn't be done, but they did it.

More than 50,000 people greeted them at Edwards Air Force Base when they returned from flying 26,000 miles without refueling. They faced some anxious moments when an electrical pump, used to draw fuel from the tank, failed. Jeana also suffered from bruises when she was tossed into the cabin wall and ceiling from unexpected turbulence. But they made it ahead of schedule.

Mobil Corporation provided the synthetic oil for what they described as the toughest test in history. The company bought a full-page ad in *USA Today* congratulating Yeager and Rutan and promoting their product. The ad closed with these words: "We believed it could be done, but you, Dick and Jeana, proved it. *And doing beats talking every time.*"

Until we're willing to act, our words are not going to mean very much. People would rather see what we do than hear what we say.

Loving Is Dangerous

C.S. Lewis wrote, "To love at all is to be vulnerable. Love anything and your heart will certainly be wrung and possibly be broken." Then he concluded, "The only place outside of heaven where you can be perfectly safe from the danger of love is hell."

Lewis is not talking about love as we have reduced it in common language. We love everything from cheesecake to fried zucchini. But love is a relational word—personal and interpersonal. It involves risk and a willingness to be vulnerable.

In relationships there is usually a price to pay. When we love, what hurts another hurts us; what brings them sorrow brings us tears. What causes them anxiety makes our hearts beat faster.

If you want to be safe from pain, don't love. But if you want to be human, go ahead and accept the fact that you *have to* love, even though love is dangerous.

Have a Goal in Sight

Our commitment is diminished when we lose sight of our goals. Florence Chadwick tried to swim the English Channel some years ago, and she almost made it. In fact, she asked to be taken out of the water just a few hundred yards from the shore she was trying to reach.

The people who had watched her courageous attempts asked her, "Why couldn't you make it? You had swum for miles. Why didn't you make those last few yards?"

"I would have made it," she answered, "but a fog bank moved in, and I couldn't see the shore."

We need goals, a purpose in life. Even our energy runs out if we can't see our destination.

1,900 Things that Won't Run

Thomas Edison had been working all day and into the night, trying to uncover the secret that would help him invent the light bulb—to no avail. He had been working for months and months on that project with no apparent success.

As Edison came out of his lab late one evening, he looked exhausted. A friend who met him there asked, "How many experiments have you done already?"

"More than 1,900," Edison replied.

"More than 1,900!" exclaimed the colleague. "That's incredible. You must feel very disappointed by now, very much a failure."

Edison straightened to his full stature, and his eyes glistened. "Not at all," he said. "I don't feel like a failure. I've made so much progress. You see, I now know more than 1,900 things that won't work. One of these days I'm going to hit on the one that does."

That's what it means to live with persistence and expectation. It's also what it means to live by faith.

Playing It Safe

I remember the first time I capsized my small sailboat. I screwed up my courage and decided to see just how much I could get out of her. I was amazed and thrilled, even though I ended up in the lake struggling with my friend to right her again.

Since then I have been frightened while sailing but not frightened of the boat. I know her, and I know that capsizing is not the worst thing that can happen to you. Until I was willing to risk capsizing I robbed myself of much of the joy of sailing.

Playing it safe may have merit in some situations but as a lifestyle it is very limiting.

We miss the richness of new friendships, new discoveries in faith, new opportunities to serve others, new possibilities for joy and adventure.

The problem with most of us is that we prefer the hell of a predictable situation rather than risk the joy of an unpredictable one.

Rocking Chairs Get You Nowhere

As a communication device, bumper stickers do the job. Whether we like them or not, they work. They get our attention, and that's effective communication.

I saw one recently which said, "Worry is like a rocking chair . . . it's something to do but it won't get you anywhere."

That's partially true.

I'd like to suggest a radical departure from those who are making millions writing books about overcoming worry or prescribing medicine to mellow us out in our stress. My idea is to keep on worrying but worry about things that matter. Worry creatively and be spurred to action about starving children and homeless families and inadequate public education. Worry about young people being taught that economic success is the secret to happiness. Worry and do something about TV advertising that associates the good life with alcohol.

There's truth in the slogan, "Worry is like a rocking chair." But we could change it. We could use our worries to get us somewhere.

Attitudes, Not Circumstances

The circumstances of our lives are never as important as our attitudes toward those circumstances. Laurel Lee is the would-be victim of Hodgkin's Disease who has demonstrated this fact. She has written at least two books, both recording her feelings, thoughts and observations as she has walked through the valley of the shadow of death.

She likened the choices of life to standing before a button panel. "You push the down-button for bitterness, resentment and self-pity. Or you can push the up-button and draw closer to God, closer to others and be a better person. It's always an act of the will, a will beyond emotions or what you feel like doing. You can be deceived by feelings."

Choosing is crucial—deciding to push the up-button of life.

What we need to remember is that the circumstances of our lives are never as important as our attitudes toward those circumstances.

Please, Just Go Back Home

A teenage boy walked into a cafe and sat down. "I'm hungry but I don't have any money. If you'll feed me, I'll be glad to wash dishes."

While the cook prepared the meal, he asked the boy to tell him his story. The teenager told him that he had argued with his father, and it got so bad that he left home.

Then the cook said to him, "You know, your story is similar to my son's. We got mad a few months ago and said a lot of angry things. I'd give anything to take back those things now. But my son is gone and I have no idea where he is. I own this cafe; it's not much, but I'd gladly give it up to have my son back home." Then he added, "You have a father back home, and I imagine he feels about like I do. Why don't you go back home?"

I don't know who you are estranged from today—wife, husband, parent, children. My hunch is they would like to have you come back home. Why don't you go?